the BIG PICTURE

Living Your Life in Light of Eternity

MAC HAMMOND

09 08 07 06 05 10 9 8 7 6 5 4 3 2 1

The Big Picture
Living Your Life in Light of Eternity
ISBN 978-1-57399-414-9
Copyright © 2012 by Mac Hammond

Published by Mac Hammond Ministries
PO Box 29469
Minneapolis, MN 55429

Contents

Section 1

Identifying the Big Picture

Chapter 1

The Puzzle Pieces of Life

Imagine for a moment that you had a thousand-piece puzzle scattered on your living room floor, but someone threw away the box top. Would you want to even attempt to put the puzzle together? Sure, you could put it together by matching the colors and shapes of each piece to create the full picture, but it would take hours and possibly never get done. It's much easier to put the puzzle together when you have the box top. Why? Because when you can see the whole picture, the smaller pieces fall into place much more quickly.

Have you ever felt like life was like that puzzle? Ever felt like hundreds of funny-shaped cardboard pieces were lying at your feet and you had no idea where to put them? Or perhaps you feel you are one of the funny-shaped pieces lying face down in a pile of scrambled puzzle pieces, and you hope someone will find where you fit in the big picture of life?

You're not alone. Most people around the world have wondered, *What is the purpose of life? Why am I really here?* These questions are truly unanswerable if you can't see the box top, or what I like to call the big picture of life.

God has a master plan for mankind that started before the world began and will last into the eternal ages to come.

You play a vital role in that plan, not just here on earth but also into eternity. When you have a larger context of understanding God's big picture as it relates to the eternal ages past into the eternal ages to come, the puzzle pieces of your life will begin to make a lot more sense. And that's why I want to show you the box top of life: how to find it, what it looks like, and how it affects your life today.

Chapter 2

Finding the Right Box Top

You will get a dozen different answers if you ask any dozen Christians to fill in this blank: "The purpose of life is…." Evangelism, missions, prayer, worship, redemption, leadership, faith, Bible study—the list of possible answers will be as varied as the number of Christians around the world!

Most Christians will fill in the blank with what is the strongest desire in their own hearts, yet none of their answers would be quite right. It might be the emphasis God has given them for their individual lives, but that doesn't mean it's the overall picture for mankind. You've heard the expression "He couldn't see the forest for the trees." That applies particularly well in this situation. People have the tendency to become so focused on a particular issue or desire that they lose sight of the larger context of God's purpose.

All of these smaller pictures that people have for their individual lives are only snapshots of God's big picture for mankind.

The Secular Viewpoint

If you ask non-Christians what the big picture of life looks like, you'll get another wide variety of answers. Some people might quote Howard Nordberg and say, "Life is a cement trampoline." Others may agree more with Roberts Byrne and say, "The purpose of life is a life of purpose." And eternal pessimists may quote Abraham Cowley, "Life is an incurable disease."

Most non-Christians end up turning to various religions or philosophies to find answers. Atheists and agnostics suggest that the experience of life is birth and death—period. Existentialists say you can create your own meaning of life. Hindus aim for a well-lived life of righteousness. A Buddhist's goal is nirvana, a state of freedom from suffering. Other religious persuasions say the purpose of life is an enlightened soul or the attainment of perfect mental peace.

When considering these various pictures of life, it's important to note that all of them can be traced back to the mind of a man. Every religion and philosophy on this earth today—save for Christianity—came from the mind of a man or woman, someone as fallible and prone to error as you and me.

I don't know about you, but I'd prefer to base my life on something more certain than man's opinion, especially when it comes to eternal issues. How can a mere mortal ever fully know what lies on the other side of death? No natural intellect could ever comprehend eternity, much less the vastness of God, the reality of Satan, or the authenticity of the two.

If no man can understand or determine these things, why would you want to base your life on a man's opinion? I'd rather have a reference point regarding eternal things that transcends human opinion—a solid, proven reference point that shows us why we are here on this earth today.

Only one such reference point exists: the Bible.

The Box Top of the Bible

The Bible is the only reference on earth that did not originate from the mind of man. It came to us over thousands of years through hundreds of prophets and scribes. It provides a perfect picture of God's eternal purpose for man and for creation. It gives us understanding of the eternal ages past all the way into the eternal ages to come.

God even provided a way we can verify the Bible—Bible prophecy. God didn't fill the Bible with prophecy just to keep us entertained or to inspire us a little here and there; the primary reason for Bible prophecy is to authenticate the divine origins of the Bible. And that's exactly what it does. The unfolding record of history continues to validate the authenticity of the Bible as one prophetic utterance after another comes to pass.

If we're ever going to have a correct picture or paradigm of life, it's going to have to begin with the truth we find in the Bible.

I want to clarify that I'm talking about the whole Bible, not just part of it. When you look at the box top of the Bible, you can't pick and choose what part of the Bible you want to believe. You have to accept the Word of God in its entirety as a revelation of three things: the person of God, the plan of God, and the place in His plan that you have. These three truths are literal, unchanging, and eternal, and you have to accept them as just that in your life.

Too many people believe what they want to believe regarding the Word of God. "I'll believe in healing, but that prosperity talk is a little too much." Or "I'll believe that I'll go to heaven after I leave this earth, but I'm not sure what I think about the Rapture."

Whenever you start picking and choosing what you want to believe (whether intentionally or unintentionally), you become the creator. You're creating your own religion and belief system by intellectually defining a God that is acceptable to you—and that's not one that exists! The God that is revealed in the Bible is the true God, and you have to accept all of what He says or nothing at all.

So what is the big picture of life that the Bible presents? Let's find out.

Section 2

Glimpses of the Big Picture

Chapter 3

Where It All Began

A little girl once asked her mother, "How did the human race come about?"

The mother answered, "God made Adam and Eve; they had children and so all mankind was made."

A few days later, the little girl asked her father the same question. The father answered, "Many years ago there were monkeys, and we developed from them."

The confused girl returned to her mother and said, "Mom, how is it possible that you told me the human race was created by God and Dad says we developed from monkeys?"

The mother answered, "Well, dear, it is very simple. I told you about the origin of my side of the family, and your father told you about his side."

Although it's only a joke (and I do love a good joke!), this reminds me of the evident polarity of opinions regarding when this universe came into existence. Creation, evolution, the big bang theory—which one is right?

Science and the Bible

Let me first point out that science and the Bible are not irrevocably different. Many people assume there is an unchangeable chasm between scientific theory and religious thought. But the truth is, when rightly divided, science and the Bible truly do corroborate one another.

Science in itself is a good thing; it can be defined as a body of data arrived at and validated by repeated experimentation and observation. God wants us to reason, observe, and properly draw conclusions that lead us to the truth. Isaiah 1:18 says, "Come now, and let us reason together, saith the Lord: though your sins be as scarlet, they shall be as white as snow; though they be red like crimson, they shall be as wool." Our God-given rational capacity will take us to salvation and blessing if we begin with the right premise: God and His Word.

Reason is the heart and essence of science. Your rational capacity will lead you to God; it will stabilize and establish you in the faith and give you a basis of information with which to convince others of the same.

Science and the Bible, when properly understood, work together to help paint the bigger picture of our earth and its history. So when a question arises between the two, a correct answer must be available that agrees with both science and the Bible.

The Fallacy of Evolution

I do need to clarify that some science should be ignored; Paul warned Timothy in 1 Timothy 6:20 not to be moved or deceived by false science. There are some things that have come out of the scientific field that really haven't been the result of the empirical process. They have little to do with experimentation or observation, which proper science is based upon. We need to be aware of this distinction because false science and the Bible will contradict each other.

A great example of false science is evolution. It is a theory that has never been supported by experimentation or observation. It says that you and I came from a single-cell amoeba that gradually evolved into you. Evolutionists believe ionized and magnetized particles of dust in the void of space were drawn together, compacted, and began to revolve and rotate. Over billions of years, these particles evolved into solar systems, suns, planets, etc. Humanity eventually came into existence through this same evolutionary process.

The problem with this theory is that it has absolutely no empirical value; most scientists have discounted this theory because of it. One reason is because it violates the first and second laws of thermodynamics. The first law of thermodynamics states that "no one can create or destroy energy. There always is, always was, and probably always will be the same total amount of energy in the universe—exactly 100 percent—and that's all we have to work with."[1]

The second law of thermodynamics gives the idea that "every naturally occurring transformation of energy is accompanied, somewhere, by a loss in the availability of energy for the future performance of work. … For this reason, no process can be 100% efficient, with all of the available energy converted in to work. Some [energy] must be deployed to overcome friction and will be degraded to nonrecoverable heat energy, which will finally be radiated into space and dispersed."[2]

Evolution couldn't have happened as they suggest it did. It relies on a constant increase of energy, which couldn't be possible according to these two scientifically proven laws. That's why most scientists adopt the big bang theory of creation.

What Was the "Big Bang"?

Scientists who believe in the big bang theory say the world had a very clear beginning around 15 to 20 billion years ago. They don't really know how to describe what happened, except to say that it started with a "big bang."

Looking at this in light of scriptural truths, I'd like to suggest that "big bang" wasn't an explosion of natural particles haphazardly coming together. Nothing natural could have initiated the bang because nothing existed at that point; it had to have a supernatural origin. And what better explanation than to look back to what the Bible says:

In the beginning God created the heaven and the earth.
Genesis 1:1

In my estimation, the big bang theory isn't in conflict with God's Word. Genesis 1:1 could very easily refer to the big bang that many people assume took place. God spoke. Creation was. There was a definite start to creation, just as the big bang experts have theorized. Plus, I think a supernatural answer is truly the only possible origin for creation that anyone can give.

What Is the Earth's Age?

But what about the age of the earth? If Genesis 1:1 really does refer to the big bang like I'm suggesting it does, that means it happened billions of years ago, which is contrary to the time period many Christians give to creation. How can that difference be explained?

Well, genealogical records of Scripture do date Adam's creation back to around 6,000 years ago. But based on scriptures such as 2 Peter 3:8 and Daniel 9:24-27, we can see that God's days are much different than our days. Do we really know exactly how much time passed during the week of creation we see accounted for in Genesis 1?

In addition to that, there's a nuance in the translation of Genesis 1:2 that gives even more room for the fact that the earth could be billions of years old:

> And the earth was without form, and void; and darkness was upon the face of the deep. And the Spirit of God moved upon the face of the waters.

Most people take this verse at face value, but if we study it a little further, we'll find something interesting. The Hebrew word for "without form" is *tohu*.[3] That word is also used in Isaiah 45:18:

> For thus saith the Lord that created the heavens; God himself that formed the earth and made it; he hath established it, he created it not in vain, he formed it to be inhabited: I am the Lord; and there is none else.

The phrase "in vain" is the same word *tohu* used in Genesis 1:2. That means Genesis 1:1-2 says God created the world and it was without form and void, and Isaiah 45:18 says that He created it with form and without void.

How can we explain this difference?

We can explain it by looking at the Hebrew verb for "was" in Genesis 1:2—*hayah*. No other place in the Bible is this Hebrew verb *hayah* translated as "was." Five hundred other times in the Old Testament, this verb is translated as "became" or "becamest."[4] If we translated *hayah* in Genesis 1:2 as "became," which is consistent with the way the verb is defined throughout the Bible, the verse would then read, "The earth became without form and void." My guess is the King James translators couldn't wrap their minds around what was being said conceptually if Genesis 1:2 was translated as "became." So they decided to translate it as "was."

Don't be alarmed. I'm not changing Scripture. I'm using the Word to interpret itself. Remember, translations of the Bible are not divinely inspired. The "infallible Word of God" refers to the prophets who first spoke God's Word into this earth. Bible scholars bring their own prejudices to their work. The people who translated the Bible into the King James Version worked within their own natural understanding of the Bible while translating it.

If the earth became without form and void, God must have created the world to have form, just as Isaiah 45:18 said. That also means something happened between Genesis 1:1 and Genesis 1:2 to cause the world to lose the form and void God had given it. What was it?

A Look Back to Fill in the Gap

God gave some of the Old Testament prophets a look back into what these events of the dateless past were. Look at Ezekiel 28:12:

> *Son of man, take up a lamentation upon the king of Tyrus, and say unto him, Thus saith the Lord God; Thou sealest up the sum, full of wisdom, and perfect in beauty.*

Most people assume Ezekiel is talking to the king of Tyrus, but that's not entirely accurate. If you'll read the rest of the verse, you'll actually see that couldn't be right. The king of Tyrus didn't seal up the sum of all wisdom; he wasn't perfect in beauty. No man has ever met that description. What is happening here is something called the law of double reference, which is common in the Bible. For example, Jesus once turned to Peter and said, "Get thee behind me, Satan" (Matthew 16:23). Did Peter suddenly turn into Satan? No. Jesus was addressing the spirit that was prompting Peter at that moment. The same type of thing is going on in Ezekiel.

Who then is he talking to? Look at verse 13:

> *Thou hast been in Eden the garden of God; every precious stone was thy covering, the sardius, topaz, and the diamond, the beryl, the onyx, and the jasper, the sapphire, the emerald, and the carbuncle, and gold: the workmanship of thy tabrets and of thy pipes was prepared in thee in the day that thou wast created.*

This is describing Lucifer in the Garden of Eden. Since this wasn't his condition when he showed up to tempt Eve, this refers to a time before Adam showed up. So even though Ezekiel was naturally speaking to the king of Tyrus, he was actually addressing the spirit behind the king of Tyrus, who happened to be Satan or Lucifer.

In verse 14, we find out why Satan was there in the Garden of Eden:

> *Thou art the anointed cherub that covereth; and*
> *I have set thee so....*

God is an orderly God. When He creates, He sets up and establishes levels of authority, organization, and rulership throughout His creation. At the time this Scripture is referring to, God used the angelic hosts to do that. There are different orders and levels of angels such as cherubs and seraphim; archangels are the ruling angels and the highest level of authority in the kingdom of God.

Of the three archangels, Lucifer was one. Lucifer had rulership responsibility; he was anointed to "cover." God had anointed him to manage this segment of God's creation. We also know from verse 13 that he was a musician ("the workmanship of thy tabrets and of thy pipes") and had the responsibility of leading the hosts of heaven in praise and worship of the Lord. He was described as the Lord's most beautiful of all creation and was headquartered on the planet earth.

Verse 14 continues:

> *...thou wast upon the holy mountain of God;*
> *thou hast walked up and down in the midst of the*
> *stones of fire. Thou wast perfect in thy ways from*

*the day thou wast created, till iniquity was found in
thee. By the multitude of thy merchandise they have
filled the midst of thee with violence, and thou hast
sinned: therefore I will cast thee as profane out of the
mountain of God: and I will destroy thee, O covering
cherub, from the midst of the stones of fire. Thine
heart was lifted up because of thy beauty, thou hast
corrupted thy wisdom by reason of thy brightness: I
will cast thee to the ground, I will lay thee before
kings, that they may behold thee.*

Ezekiel 28:14-17

We see more about this in Isaiah 14:12-14:

*How art thou fallen from heaven, O Lucifer, son
of the morning! how art thou cut down to the ground,
which didst weaken the nations! For thou hast said in
thine heart, I will ascend into heaven, I will exalt my
throne above the stars of God: I will sit also upon the
mount of the congregation, in the sides of the north:
I will ascend above the heights of the clouds; I will
be like the most High.*

Lucifer was so caught up in his own beauty that he
decided (very much like Adam did) to elevate his status
to that of God. And, as you know, he led one third of the
angelic hosts in rebellion against God. God, of course,
defeated that rebellion. Verse 15 says, "Yet thou shalt be
brought down to hell, to the sides of the pit."

Isaiah 14:17 shows us that his downfall brought chaos
to the world: "That made the world as a wilderness, and
destroyed the cities thereof."

Jeremiah 4:23 gives us another glimpse into this catastrophe of Satan's fall:

> *I beheld the earth, and, lo, it was without form, and void; and the heavens, and they had no light.*

That's the same word *tohu* that we've seen twice already in Genesis 1:2 and Isaiah 45:18. In Jeremiah chapter 4, Jeremiah is seeing the earth as it was after Lucifer's fall:

> *I beheld the earth, and, lo, it was without form, and void; and the heavens, and they had no light. I beheld the mountains, and, lo, they trembled, and all the hills moved lightly. I beheld, and, lo, there was no man, and all the birds of the heavens were fled. I beheld, and, lo, the fruitful place was a wilderness, and all the cities thereof were broken down at the presence of the Lord, and by his fierce anger.*
>
> Jeremiah 4:23-26

Lucifer's rebellion had such a cataclysmic impact on earth that it literally destroyed life on the earth at that time, and the earth became without form and void. Never again will the earth be made without form and void by the Lord's fierce anger. This is the only time it happened.

Now, did you see that Isaiah and Jeremiah both mention nations and cities that existed before Adam ever came on the scene? Something called man had walked the earth—a creature who most likely appeared as we do but wasn't made in God's image and likeness. (That didn't occur until Adam was created, as noted in Genesis 1:27.) If nations lived prior to Lucifer's fall, we can assume animals did as well.

When you realize that life existed before God's re-creation as accounted for in Genesis, you'll see plenty of room in the Bible for the fossil record which scientists often say disproves the validity of the Bible. I mean, these nations may have lived for millions of years prior to being destroyed by Lucifer's fall. There's room prior to Lucifer's rebellion for dinosaurs, all kinds of prehistoric animal life, and even human life such as the Neanderthal man and the Cro-Magnon man. God Himself told Adam in Genesis 1:28 to:

> *Be fruitful, and multiply, and replenish the earth, and subdue it: and have dominion over the fish of the sea, and over the fowl of the air, and over every living thing that moveth upon the earth.*

"Replenish" the earth. God didn't say "plenish" the earth for the first time. He said replenish it. It had already been populated with life! How long was there life on earth before Lucifer's fall? We don't know, but given the scientific records, I think it's completely appropriate to assume all of this took place billions of years ago. Why? Because when scientific facts and biblical truths are viewed correctly, they corroborate one another and are just another example of the magnitude and majesty of the God that we serve.

This is how the world began: both the creation and re-creation accounts that the Bible tells us about. Let's take a look at what happened next.

Chapter 4

The Seven Human Dispensations

God's dealings with man over the next 6,000 years of recorded history can be viewed in seven dispensations of time. A dispensation is simply a term for a time period during which God relates to humankind in a particular way in order to promote right decision making on mankind's part. Each of these seven dispensations of mankind lead up to and prepare man for the eternal ages to come. Let me walk you through what each of these dispensations are.

The first dispensation of man is called the dispensation of innocence. It began when Adam was created and ended when Adam fell. During this timeframe, man in his innocence walked with God in the cool of the garden. There was no inhibition to his relationship with the Lord because he had no knowledge of the difference between good and evil.

After Adam's fall, the Lord gave man his conscience which enabled him to ascertain the difference between right and wrong. This was the dispensation of human conscience. This dispensation of conscience continued until the time of Noah's flood, when the dispensation of civil government began. God began to direct the standard of behavior for mankind through the civil law, a legislated method by which good would be chosen as opposed to evil.

The dispensation of human government ran from Noah's flood until the call of Abram out of the Ur of the Chaldees when Abram was 70 years old. At that point, the dispensation of promise began, and God entered into covenant with man for the first time and chose to express Himself through that covenant relationship with His chosen people. Faith became a factor in the way God dealt with mankind.

This period lasted until the time of Moses, when God gave man the law or the Word of God. At this point, the dispensation of the law began. Through Moses and later the Levitical priesthood, God's laws described man's behavior within the framework (hopefully) of good. This dispensation of the law is also known as the Jewish dispensation. This dispensation hasn't actually ended. It has been temporarily suspended while the sixth dispensation takes place.

This sixth dispensation is the time period we are in currently; it is often called the church age or the dispensation of grace. This is the time when salvation has been made available by grace through faith in Jesus. It's also referred to as the dispensation of the Holy Spirit because this is the time period when the Holy Spirit is poured out on the Church.

Some controversies exist as to when the church age actually began. Answers vary from the birth of Jesus to when Jesus was baptized by John the Baptist to Jesus' death and resurrection to the day of Pentecost. In our persuasion of faith, we endorse the latter belief as the most scriptural perspective for the beginning of the church age.

The Hidden Dispensation

Now the church age is an interesting dispensation because the Lord intended that it be kept a secret. Old Testament prophets saw directly across the church age to the second advent of Christ; Old Testament prophecy had nothing to do with the church age. Paul talks about this in Ephesians 3:1-6:

> For this cause I Paul, the prisoner of Jesus Christ for you Gentiles, If ye have heard of the dispensation of the grace of God which is given me to you-ward: how that by revelation he made known unto me the mystery; (as I wrote afore in few words, whereby, when ye read, ye may understand my knowledge in the mystery of Christ) which in other ages was not made known unto the sons of men, as it is now revealed unto his holy apostles and prophets by the Spirit; that the Gentiles should be fellowheirs, and of the same body, and partakers of his promise in Christ by the gospel:

Why did the Lord want this to be a secret? We see the answer in 1 Corinthians 2:7-8:

> But we speak the wisdom of God in a mystery, even the hidden wisdom, which God ordained before the world unto our glory: which none of the princes of this world knew: for had they known it, they would not have crucified the Lord of glory.

The very purpose of the church age is to preach the Gospel to all the world, which clearly goes against Satan's plan. If Satan had known that Jesus was going to be raised from the dead as the firstborn of many to come, if he had any idea that there were going to be multitudes walking around filled with the Holy Spirit and His power to change this world for God, he would have never crucified our Lord. That's why the church age was kept a mystery.

The church age is tucked in between the 69th and 70th weeks that Daniel talks about in Daniel chapter 9. When the church age is over (the Church is caught away in the Rapture), the Jewish dispensation or the dispensation of the law has one week of years (seven years) before it's completed. This period, also known as the Tribulation, will experience the greatest outpouring of God's wrath on a level that mankind has never experienced before in all of earth's history.

After the Tribulation is complete, the Second Advent of Jesus Christ and the battle of Armageddon will take place (Revelation 19:11-21). Once that's complete, the establishment of the seventh dispensation of man will begin, which is the dispensation of divine government (Revelation 20:1-5), better known as the millennial reign of our Lord. It will last for 1,000 years after the return of Jesus.

These are the seven dispensations of man that will take place between the eternal ages past and the eternal ages to come. All of them are preparation for the destiny God has prepared for us during eternity. Let's take a look now at exactly what that destiny is, where we are currently in the plan of God, and what happens between now and the time we'll be walking in our eternal destiny.

Chapter 5

The End of This Age

At this very moment, you and I are living at the end of the church age. We're within a short time period of the Rapture of the Church.

Some people find this hard to believe. "Ever since I was young, my grandmamma has been saying, 'Jesus is going to come back any day now,' but He still hasn't showed up yet!"

It's true. Throughout Church history, people have been saying the Lord will be coming back at any minute, but He hasn't yet, and I think many have lost sense of the urgency because of it. They've become tired of hearing it, even to the point where they doubt the truth of it.

Peter knew people would have this attitude. He wrote in 2 Peter 3:3-7:

> *Knowing this first, that there shall come in the last days scoffers, walking after their own lusts….*

I would certainly say this describes our society today. We've got a generation of scoffers and mockers who deride the truth of God's Word like we've never seen before. They are itching to pursue their own agendas and fulfill the lusts of their own flesh. It is one of the signs of the times that we live in.

... and saying, Where is the promise of his coming? for since the fathers fell asleep, all things continue as they were from the beginning of the creation. For this they willingly are ignorant of, that by the word of God the heavens were of old, and the earth standing out of the water and in the water: whereby the world that then was, being overflowed with water, perished: but the heavens and the earth, which are now, by the same word are kept in store, reserved unto fire against the day of judgment and perdition of ungodly men.

verses 3-7

This isn't talking about Noah's flood, but rather a time when people are willingly ignorant of the message of Scripture that tells us about earth's history beyond the re-creation event in Genesis, which gives us a perspective on where we are in God's scheme of things. These verses precede verse 8:

But, beloved, be not ignorant of this one thing, that one day is with the Lord as a thousand years, and a thousand years as one day.

You and I must understand the times and seasons of the end of this age if we don't want to become a scoffer. And in order to properly understand the times and seasons, we need to know that a thousand years is as a day and a day is as a thousand years. (Don't apply this principle every time you see the phrase "one day" in the Bible. If you do that, you're going to be hopelessly confused. This principle only relates to end time prophecy which helps us determine what day we're living in.)

A Prophetic Preview

With this truth in mind, we can see numerous prophetic snapshots in the Word of God, both in the Old Testament and New Testament, which clearly show us that the day you and I live in is toward the end of the church age. I want to show you just a few.

In Luke 10:30-35, Jesus told the parable of the Good Samaritan. For years, Sunday school teachers have taught that this parable means you should help someone who is hurting, even if it inconveniences you. But it holds another layer of meaning deeper than simply being a good-deed doer. Let's look at it in light of scriptural typology. Luke 10:30 says:

> *And Jesus answering said, A certain man went down from Jerusalem to Jericho, and fell among thieves, which stripped him of his raiment, and wounded him, and departed, leaving him half dead.*

In Scripture, Jerusalem is always a type of the heavenly and Jericho is always a type of the earthly. The thieves referenced who attacked this man are a type of Satan and his demonic hosts. (Jesus referred to Satan in John 10:10 as the thief who comes to kill, steal, and destroy.)

So a man coming from heaven to earth fell among Satan and his satanic hosts. Does that sound familiar? It's a parallel to Adam, someone made in the image and likeness of God, with heavenly origins, who was fit for living on earth. However, he fell among thieves—Satan and his satanic hosts, who had been cast out of heaven when their rebellion failed.

These demonic hosts stripped Adam of his raiment, which is a reference to the glory of God. They wounded him and departed, leaving him half dead. In other words, they left him spiritually dead, but biologically alive.

> *And by chance there came down a certain priest that way: and when he saw him, he passed by on the other side. And likewise a Levite, when he was at the place, came and looked on him, and passed by on the other side.*
>
> Luke 10:31-32

These verses are a clear indication of established traditional religion's inability to do anything about man's fallen condition.

Who was it who was able to help this man? "But a certain Samaritan, as he journeyed, came where he was: and when he saw him, he had compassion on him..." (verse 33). The Samaritan is a type of Jesus. What did Jesus do when He saw him?

> [He] *went to him, and bound up his wounds, pouring in oil and wine, and set him on his own beast, and brought him to an inn, and took care of him. And on the morrow when he departed, he took out two pence, and gave them to the host, and said unto him, Take care of him; and whatsoever thou spendest more, when I come again, I will repay thee.*
>
> Luke 10:34-35

Oil is a type of the Holy Spirit and the new birth. Wine is a type of the Holy Spirit and the baptism of the Holy Spirit. That's what Jesus supplied to this man before bringing him to an inn. The inn is a type of the Church because that's where those who have been left half dead by the enemy and have been ministered to by Jesus can find their growth and health return in the Lord.

The Samaritan left the man with the host, another type of the Holy Spirit, and gave the host two pence in order to take care of the man. Commentaries tell us that one day's labor was one pence. In other words, the Samaritan left him with sufficient supply for two days' worth of care. If we're looking at this in light of the end times, a day is as 1,000 years with the Lord; that means we can rephrase the verse like this: Jesus (the Good Samaritan) left the broken man at the Church (the inn) in care of the Holy Spirit (the host) with enough provision (two day's wages) for two thousand years before His return.

Why is two thousand years important? Scholars estimate the church age began around two thousand years ago. If Jesus left the man in care of the Church for 2,000 years, then the end of this age must be close.

Other Snapshots of the Church Age

Let me show you a few more snapshots that confirm the length of the church age is two thousand years long. Look at Luke 2:42-43:

And when [Jesus] was twelve years old, they went up to Jerusalem after the custom of the feast. And when they had fulfilled the days, as they returned, the child Jesus tarried behind in Jerusalem; and Joseph and his mother knew not of it.

Before you get too hard on Joseph and Mary for leaving Jesus behind, let me assure you, we've had plenty of parents who have left their kids in our grade school ministry by accident!

Let's read on.

But they, supposing him to have been in the company, went a day's journey; and they sought him among their kinsfolk and acquaintance. And when they found him not, they turned back again to Jerusalem, seeking him. And it came to pass, that after three days they found him in the temple, sitting in the midst of the doctors, both hearing them, and asking them questions.

Luke 2:44-46

Jesus was separated from His own flesh and blood for two days, a day out and a day back. In a larger sense, His flesh and blood represent the Jewish people. In other words, Jesus left the Jews for two days or 2,000 years before they found Him again in the temple at the end of that time.

Do you see the parallel between the Jewish dispensation temporarily ending for the church age to take place?

We see this same reference in John chapter 4 when Jesus was ministering to the Samaritan woman. After talking with Jesus, she went back to her town and invited the people of her city to come listen to Jesus. Look at what happened.

> *And many of the Samaritans of that city believed on him for the saying of the woman, which testified, He told me all that ever I did. So when the Samaritans were come unto him, they besought him that he would tarry with them: and he abode there two days.*
>
> John 4:39-40

The Samaritans are a Gentile people. Jesus redirected his ministry from the Jews to the Gentiles for two days. After two days, he returned to the Jews.

Let me show you one last snapshot. This example is in the Old Testament in Hosea chapter 6:

> *Come, and let us return unto the Lord: for he hath torn, and he will heal us; he hath smitten, and he will bind us up. After two days will he revive us: in the third day he will raise us up, and we shall live in his sight.*
>
> Hosea 6:1-2

Do you see the parallel? The Jews will be revived after two days or two thousand years, and in that third day, "he will raise us up, and we shall live in his sight." It's a prophetic utterance regarding the millennial reign of our Lord when the Jews will be God's emissaries on earth. (I'll talk about that further in a later chapter.)

These snapshots are just a few of those given throughout the Word, and they all tell the same thing: the end of this age is here.

When Will It Happen?

Now, we can't pinpoint the exact day this age will end. For starters, as I've mentioned, we don't know exactly when it started. Secondly, there's a difference between the Jewish lunar calendar and our solar calendar, which could make a difference of a few years as well. But most importantly, Jesus tells us in Matthew 24:36, "But of that day and hour knoweth no man, no, not the angels of heaven, but my Father only." (If someone tells you that Jesus is going to return next year on January 31 at two in the afternoon, forget it. He's a flake and doesn't know what he's talking about!)

But whether you measure from Jesus' birth, ministry, death, resurrection, or from the day of Pentecost, two thousand years of time are close to fulfillment. We are certainly in the season where these prophetic snapshots are going to be fulfilled. We can not only determine that from the timeline we've talked about, but we can also see it through various passages of Scripture.

Matthew 24:32-35 says:

From the fig tree learn this lesson: as soon as its young shoots become soft and tender and it puts out its leaves, you know of a surety that summer is near. So also when you see these signs, all taken together, coming to pass, you may know of a surety that He is near, at the very doors. Truly I tell you, this genera-

tion (the whole multitude of people living at the
same time, in a definite, given period) will not pass
away till all these things taken together take place.
Sky and earth will pass away, but My words will not
pass away. (Amp.)

Israel, which is represented by the fig tree, has been
dispersed across the world for 2,000 years. This Scripture
refers to the time when they will be gathered together again
as a nation. The generation that is alive and sees this happen
shall not pass until all these things have been fulfilled.

In 70 AD, the Roman Emperor Titus destroyed
Jerusalem and the temple and scattered the Jews throughout
the world. For years, they lived without a homeland. But in
1948, the world of nations recognized the formation of the
nation of Israel. Since then, Jews have begun coming back
to their homeland from all over the world. I am part of the
generation that saw this happen; so just as this Scripture
says, I fully believe my generation will not pass away until
we see the return of our Lord Jesus.

Another sign of the end of the times is found in
2 Timothy 3:1-5:

This know also, that in the last days perilous times
shall come. For men shall be lovers of their own selves,
covetous, boasters, proud, blasphemers, disobedient to
parents, unthankful, unholy, without natural affec-
tion, trucebreakers, false accusers, incontinent, fierce,
despisers of those that are good, traitors, heady, high-
minded, lovers of pleasures more than lovers of God;
having a form of godliness, but denying the power
thereof: from such turn away.

Our society is filled with people who fit this description. They love pleasure more than they love God. They are lovers of self, proud, unthankful, despisers of good—and they're not afraid to flaunt their rebellion.

We are truly living in these end times.

The Rapture of the Church

So if we are in the end times, how will we know when the church age actually ends? Well, it ends with the Rapture of the Church. Paul writes in 1 Thessalonians 4:14-18:

> *For if we believe that Jesus died and rose again, even so them also which sleep in Jesus will God bring with him. For this we say unto you by the word of the Lord, that we which are alive and remain unto the coming of the Lord shall not prevent them which are asleep. For the Lord himself shall descend from heaven with a shout, with the voice of the archangel, and with the trump of God: and the dead in Christ shall rise first: then we which are alive and remain shall be caught up together with them in the clouds, to meet the Lord in the air: and so shall we ever be with the Lord. Wherefore comfort one another with these words.*

I like to think about what this day will look like. Graves popping open, Christians around the world leaving this earth—can you imagine the stir that's going to cause? In fact, I think the Rapture may be the trigger for the end-time harvest of souls that many people have talked about. What else would affect the world in such an enormous way than having hundreds of millions of people completely disappear? I know a lot of people would immediately get their lives right if they found themselves stuck on earth after the Rapture had taken place, facing the Tribulation. Not exactly what people would call a good time!

But, Mac, I thought the harvest of souls would come before the Rapture?

Yes, the end of this age is going to carry with it the greatest outpouring of God's Spirit, the most awesome revival and harvest that the world has ever seen. I'm excited that we get to be participants in this Holy Spirit time of revival. As James 5:7-8 says:

> Be patient therefore, brethren, unto the coming of the Lord. Behold, the husbandman waiteth for the precious fruit of the earth, and hath long patience for it, until he receive the early and latter rain. Be ye also patient; stablish your hearts: for the coming of the Lord draweth nigh.

But too many people depend on the end-time revival as their means of salvation. They think, "I'll get serious about God when the revival comes." That's a dangerous place to be. As this age comes to a close, a growing polarity will be seen between light and darkness. Jesus is coming for a bride that is pure and spotless, holy and without blemish (Ephesians 5:27). But as the Church walks in more and more light, evil will become more prevalent. Paul wrote in 2 Timothy 3:13, "But evil men and seducers shall wax worse and worse, deceiving, and being deceived."

As the last days continue, people won't be able to waver between Christianity and the secular world for much longer. They will either come down on God's side or Satan's side. If you're playing around with the world or not diligently pursuing God, you will get sucked in the wrong direction.

I know what I can and can't handle. This won't bother me. I'll still be able to walk with God, you may think.

No matter how strong you think you are, no matter how great you think your relationship with God is, no matter what excuse you can come up with, if you don't purposely choose to follow God on a daily basis, you will wind up on the world's side.

Don't wait for the revival to get serious about God; you might be waving goodbye to all your friends and remaining in the Tribulation. You can't determine the day of your salvation (John 6:44). The Rapture will come on us like a thief in the night (1 Thessalonians 5:2), so I highly suggest choosing the right way before you're stuck on this earth longer than you want to be.

This is how the church age will close—with a shout and a trump and a catching away of Christians to meet the Lord in the sky. You and I will be changed in the twinkling of an eye (1 Corinthians 15:52). What a glorious day that will be!

Chapter 6

After the Rapture

After the Rapture, the last seven years of the Jewish dispensation still need to be played out. This is commonly referred to as the Tribulation. It will be a period of time that the earth will experience the greatest outpouring of God's wrath and judgment that it has ever seen and the scales of justice will begin to be balanced. (Isaiah 26:9)

At the end of that seven years, Jesus will return to establish His earthly kingdom. This is often called the Second Advent or the Second Coming. We will return with Him for the final confrontation with Satan. The Antichrist will be defeated in the battle of Armageddon, and at that point, Satan and his demonic host will be bound and cast into the pit for a thousand years.

Where will we be during the Tribulation? First of all, after the Rapture, we'll be standing before the judgment seat of Christ. Each and every one of us will give an account for our lives. Paul writes about this in 1 Corinthians 3:10-15:

> *According to the grace of God which is given unto me, as a wise masterbuilder, I have laid the foundation, and another buildeth thereon. But let every man take heed how he buildeth thereupon. For other foundation can no man lay than that is laid, which is Jesus*

Christ. Now if any man build upon this foundation gold, silver, precious stones, wood, hay, stubble; every man's work shall be made manifest: for the day shall declare it, because it shall be revealed by fire; and the fire shall try every man's work of what sort it is. If any man's work abide which he hath built thereupon, he shall receive a reward. If any man's work shall be burned, he shall suffer loss: but he himself shall be saved; yet so as by fire.

The judgment seat of Christ is for giving out rewards for work done. All the things we have done in this life are going to be wood, hay, and stubble (evil works) burned up by the fire of God or they will be gold, silver, and precious stones (good works) that will survive the trial of fire.

We'll receive our reward after we are judged. And then we'll enjoy the marriage supper of the Lamb, a seven-year party in the heavenly arena.

Millennial Reign of the Lord

After the Tribulation, mankind will enter the millennial reign of our Lord. For the first time, men will have an opportunity to live on this earth without the evil influence of Satan.

During this time, the Jews are going to be God's emissaries upon the earth during the millennial reign. (We're not going to be here since we will have been raptured already.) Who will they be emissaries to? Look at Matthew 25:31-32:

When the Son of man shall come in his glory,
and all the holy angels with him, then shall he sit
upon the throne of his glory: and before him shall be
gathered all nations....

These are the nations of unbelievers that remain here on this earth at the end of the Tribulation.

...and he shall separate them one from another,
as a shepherd divideth his sheep from the goats: and
he shall set the sheep on his right hand, but the goats
on the left. Then shall the King say unto them on his
right hand, Come, ye blessed of my Father, inherit
the kingdom prepared for you from the foundation of
the world: (verses 32-34)

These people are not born again, but He calls them "blessed of my Father." There's only one reason for that, and we find it early on in Scripture. In Genesis 12, God made the irrevocable statement to Abram that "I will bless them that bless thee, and curse him that curseth thee (verse 3)." That promise extends to this point in time at the judgment of the living nations.

For I was an hungred, and ye gave me meat: I was
thirsty, and ye gave me drink: I was a stranger, and
ye took me in: naked, and ye clothed me: I was sick,
and ye visited me: I was in prison, and ye came unto
me. Then shall the righteous answer him, saying,
Lord, when saw we thee an hungred, and fed thee?
or thirsty, and gave thee drink? When saw we thee

41

a stranger, and took thee in? or naked, and clothed thee? Or when saw we thee sick, or in prison, and came unto thee? And the King shall answer and say unto them, Verily I say unto you, Inasmuch as ye have done it unto one of the least of these my brethren, ye have done it unto me.

Matthew 25:35-36

Every commentary I've ever read says that the phrase "the least of these my brethren" refers to the Jews. Matthew 24 continues:

Then shall he say also unto them on the left hand, Depart from me, ye cursed, into everlasting fire, prepared for the devil and his angels: for I was an hungred, and ye gave me no meat: I was thirsty, and ye gave me no drink: I was a stranger, and ye took me not in: naked, and ye clothed me not: sick, and in prison, and ye visited me not. Then shall they also answer him, saying, Lord, when saw we thee an hungred, or athirst, or a stranger, or naked, or sick, or in prison, and did not minister unto thee? Then shall he answer them, saying, Verily I say unto you, Inasmuch as ye did it not to one of the least of these, ye did it not to me. And these shall go away into everlasting punishment: but the righteous into life eternal. (verses 41-46)

Nations of people who are not born again will be ushered into the millennial reign on the basis of whether or not they've blessed Israel and the Jewish people. And

42

these are the people to whom the Jewish people will be emissaries of God's light during the millennium.

The Government of the Millennium

The millennium will be a theocracy or a divinely directed government, not only concerned with spiritual law but also with civil law. The head of that theocracy will be Jesus, the third member of the Godhead. It will be a very clearly defined governmental authority with an organizational structure similar to any government. He'll have His cabinet, advisors, lieutenants, and vice presidents, etc.

Under Jesus, King David will rule over the Jews (Israel) from Jerusalem (Jeremiah 30:9). Under King David, an apostle will be the head of each of the tribes of Israel (Luke 22:30). Under that level of authority comes the nation of Israel in general. The Jews will be God's representatives on this earth, tasked with getting the Good News out that Jesus is ruling on this earth. The nations of people who go into the millennium won't necessarily know that Jesus is there. That's why the Jews will need to spread the news of Jesus' reign and let people know about His divine laws.

Jerusalem will be the world capital (Psalm 48:1-2). Each year the nations of peoples on this earth are going to be required to send their representatives to Jerusalem to acknowledge Jesus (Isaiah 2:1-4, Zechariah 14:16-21). Civil and religious laws are going to be given to govern all nations and peoples on this earth. Very clearly defined civil and spiritual law will be given and disseminated among all peoples of the world and adherence will be enforced. (Law means nothing without a system of enforcement.) But for the first time in human history, in the enforcement of the law, both civil and spiritual, judgment and justice will be equitable. The earth will experience a just government (Isaiah 9:6-7, Isaiah 11:4), and the result will be universal peace (Psalm 72:7-9, Malachi 1:11).

The Purpose of the Millennium

What is the purpose for this time period? Well, parts of God's covenant with Abraham won't be fulfilled until the millennium, such as Abraham's seed ruling forever (2 Samuel 7:16), eternal blessing for the seed of Abraham, and the Jews occupying the land God has given them (Genesis 12:7, 17:8).

But the main purpose of this time period is to put down all rebellion and prepare the earth to be the eternal habitation of God the Father. Look at what 1 Corinthians 15:22-26 says:

> For as in Adam all die, even so in Christ shall all be made alive. But every man in his own order: Christ the firstfruits; afterward they that are Christ's at his coming. Then cometh the end, when he shall have delivered up the kingdom to God, even the Father; when he shall have put down all rule and all authority and power. For he must reign, till he hath put all enemies under his feet. The last enemy that shall be destroyed is death.

And at the end of these thousand years, Satan will be released for a short while to deceive whom he may. It's hard to believe anybody could be deceived after living with Jesus on this earth for a thousand years, but the enemy is good at his job. The Word says he will deceive many and then there will be one last final confrontation with evil

(Revelation 20:7-8). Satan will then be defeated and as Revelation 20:12-15 explains, all the dead will be raised and the Great White Throne Judgment will occur. (We won't be judged here. As I mentioned earlier, we've already been raised and judged at the judgment seat of Christ. The Great White Throne Judgment is for everyone else.) Anyone's name not written in the Lamb's Book of Life will be eternally consigned along with Satan and his demonic host to the lake of fire.

God's Relocation Plan

At the end of the Great White Throne Judgment, the earth will be renewed by fire. God will rid the earth of all corruption that has accumulated after thousands of years of man's rebellion on this earth.

After the renewal of earth by fire, God will take the capital city of heaven, New Jerusalem, and replant it on the planet earth and forever be with His man. Revelation 21:1-3 says:

> *And I saw a new heaven and a new earth: for the first heaven and the first earth were passed away; and there was no more sea. And I John saw the holy city, new Jerusalem, coming down from God out of heaven, prepared as a bride adorned for her husband. And I heard a great voice out of heaven saying, Behold, the tabernacle of God is with men, and he will dwell with them, and they shall be his people, and God himself shall be with them, and be their God.*

Thus begins the eternal ages to come.

Section 3

Your Place in the Big Picture

Chapter 7

Our Job for Eternity

Your eternal future is going to be determined by the way you live your life here on earth. I'm not talking about whether or not you'll go to heaven. If you've accepted Jesus as Lord and Savior of your life, your destiny will be heaven. But God's eternal plan doesn't leave you in heaven with nothing to do. He has a plan for you. The details of that plan are determined by how well you learn from your training on earth.

Training? Training for what? you may think.

Training for your eternal purpose. Look at Revelation 1:5-6:

> *And from Jesus Christ, the faithful witness, the firstborn from the dead, and the ruler over the kings of the earth. To Him who loved us and washed us from our sins in His own blood, and has made us kings and priests to His God and Father, to Him be glory and dominion forever and ever. Amen. (NKJV)*

One insight into understanding our eternal purpose is found in the phrase "firstborn from the dead." Jesus is "the firstborn from the dead." Well, if there is a firstborn there has to be a second born, third born, and so forth. If you have accepted Jesus as your Lord and Savior, your number is in there somewhere. You have experienced a new birth or resurrection in your spirit. Upon Jesus' return, bodily resurrection is going to follow as well, which we'll talk about a little later.

The second insight is found in the phrase "has made us kings and priests." This is past tense; it is already a done deal if you are born again. The Lord has called us to be kings and priests. What does a king do? He reigns with absolute authority, and he has every resource in his kingdom at his disposal to promote his purpose.

This is what we are going to be doing eternally. Kings are appointed for life, and since we will never die spiritually, we will rule and reign as kings with Christ forever.

Ruling and Reigning for Eternity

If we are called to be kings, we must have something to rule over. I used to think about this truth pretty narrowly. *There are some billions of believers, both past and present, who are going to reign with Christ. That must mean everybody gets two or three square feet of terra firma here on earth to rule over.*

It didn't make much sense. And then I realized that we aren't called to the earth. We're called to the universe. We're called to rule over universal creation—everything beyond this earth.

Our sun is a relatively small star in a galaxy that has billions of other stars as well as billions of other suns like ours, most of which also have planetary systems. We're just one part of the Milky Way galaxy. As our telescopes have grown stronger, we have discovered more and more nebula or galaxies. As a matter of fact, the estimates range in the billions of galaxies, each galaxy having billions of stars or suns and each of those suns having its own solar system.

Have you ever thought about the beings that populate those galaxies? I have. A lot of people would be shocked if I told them that extra-terrestrial life is part of the big picture. I still run into people who think we are the only life in this universal creation, but that's a wrong assumption. Remember what Isaiah 45:18 says? God created the world to have form and be without void. He created it to be inhabited. We are not the only creation throughout this universe; it is inhabited by other life forms. Science fiction movies will be shamed when you and I one day see the creatures the Bible talks about—the winged creatures, four-headed beasts, and angelic hosts!

I know. It's beyond our natural comprehension, but think about it for a moment. The Jews are the natural seed of Abraham and God likens them to the sand of the sea (Genesis 32:12). Then Paul wrote in Galatians 3:29, "And if ye be Christ's, then are ye Abraham's seed, and heirs according to the promise." We are the spiritual seed and likened, I believe, to the stars of the heavens which gives us a glimpse of the nature of eternal destiny—ruling and reigning with Christ over a universe whose magnitude most people really don't intellectually appreciate.

When I was a pilot in the air force, I dreamed about becoming an astronaut. I dreamed about space exploration into unknown worlds and the different things that might be found. But it was a very selective program at that point in time, and it would have taken years beyond the time I actually got off active duty to have even discovered if I could have made it. It ended up not working out for me to follow that path, so it's exciting to know I am going to represent God to all different kinds of life forms out there. I'll have plenty of time to explore space when I fulfill my eternal destiny!

We Will Represent God

Our eternal calling is a representation of a truth we see early on in the Bible in Genesis chapter 2:

> *And the Lord God took the man, and put him into the garden of Eden to dress it and to keep it.*
>
> Genesis 2:15

Adam, who was made in God's image, was created to be God's steward. A steward is one who manages and administrates on his lord's behalf. That's exactly what God asked Adam to do: keep the earth, which means to guard, hedge about, and protect.[1] God gave Adam dominion over the whole earth and commanded him to manage it on His behalf.

Now God put man on the very earth that He cast Satan back into, the same place where the rebellious angelic hosts were consigned. I don't think this was a mere coincidence or mistake. As God's stewards, we are to maintain order and bring God's commands to others. It also means that we have to learn how to deal with rebellion on this earth in preparation for our eternal calling.

Yes, rebellion will be put down forever here on earth (1 Corinthians 15:24-28, Revelation 21:27), but the Bible didn't say anything about the universe. There will be an eternal need to keep the peace because if the capacity for rebellion existed in Lucifer—another life form who had the freedom of choice—it will exist in other portions of God's universal creation. Just as we are to be peacemakers for God in this world, reconciling others to Him (2 Corinthians 5:18-20), we will be peacemakers for God on a universal scale. We will bring God's light to His universal creation and knowledge of Him to whatever life there may be out there.

You and I are in boot camp being taught how to live by the principles that will enable us to be effective for our Lord in the eternal ages to come. God placed us in this controlled environment so we can learn these lessons in a place where we can't do any universal damage. As we learn the principles of scripture, of faith, hope, and love, we are being groomed for our eternal destinies. It is all preparation for what is to come.

Every time I think about this stuff, I get amazed! The magnitude of God's plan is quite astounding.

What Will We Look Like?

If we're receiving responsibility for ruling and reigning over universal creation, we will need a body that will qualify us for the authority to do that. That's why our bodies will be glorified.

This is one of the unique things about Christianity. Most world religions teach the immortality of the spirit, not the body. But as Christians, we believe our bodies are going to be with us throughout eternity. First Corinthians 15:42-44 says:

So also is the resurrection of the dead. It is sown in corruption; it is raised in incorruption: it is sown in dishonour; it is raised in glory: it is sown in weakness; it is raised in power: it is sown a natural body; it is raised a spiritual body. There is a natural body, and there is a spiritual body.

Our bodies are going to be glorified. We'll get our new bodies when the Rapture takes place. First Corinthians 15:51-52 says, "Behold, I shew you a mystery; we shall not all sleep, but we shall all be changed, in a moment, in the twinkling of an eye, at the last trump: for the trumpet shall sound, and the dead shall be raised incorruptible, and we shall be changed."

What will our glorified bodies look like? Jesus received the first glorified body after He was raised from the dead, so let's look at some characteristics of His body.

Walking Through Walls

In Luke 24:39, Jesus mentioned that He had flesh and bones, but He didn't say anything about blood. Blood is the corrosive agent that has to be removed in the embalming process so the flesh and bones will not deteriorate. Our glorified bodies will be flesh and bone but will not have blood. (I'm not sure what we'll have flowing in our veins—perhaps the glory of God!) Our physical bodies, even though flesh and bone, will be able to pass through tangible physical material just as Jesus did when He walked through closed doors in John 20:19 and 20:26.

Eating for Pure Enjoyment

Certain things won't be required to sustain life in our glorified bodies. We'll be able to do them just because we have a physical body that has the capacity to enjoy it. For example, after His body was glorified, Jesus didn't need to eat in order to sustain life, but He ate anyway. He had a meal on the shore with His disciples after He had been glorified (John 21:12-14).

With our glorified bodies, we'll be able to eat for the pure enjoyment of eating. At the marriage supper of the Lamb, I believe my mom will be there with a pecan pie, and I'll be able to eat it just for the pure enjoyment of it. Plus, I won't need to count the calories or run an extra mile or two the next day. I'm really looking forward to that!

Sin's Effects Removed

What else do we see about a glorified body? Well, we can assume that all the effects of sin and the corruption of the sin-cursed environment will be removed. No more potbellies, receding hair lines, blemished skin, bald spots, or anything of that sort. You will still look like yourself and be able to recognize your body, but it will look better than what it looks like here on earth (1 Corinthians 15:35-38).

Faster Travel

Moving from place to place will no longer be limited to how far we can walk on our two feet or to the mode of transportation that we decide to take. Instead, we'll be able to be transported immediately to our desired destination. For example, when Jesus left this earth, He ascended to the right hand of the Father (Mark 16:19). The Lord didn't have to send a spaceship down to get Him. His body had the capacity to ascend and move across who knows how many light years of distance to planet heaven.

And yes, I did say that. Heaven is a planet. Back in Genesis 1:1, God said, "God created the heaven and the earth." The two centerpieces of God's universal creation are referred to as "the" heaven and "the" earth. Throughout the Word, heaven and earth are used synonymously when talking about creation; these two things clearly go hand in hand. I think there's a reason for that. Just as man was created in God's image to inhabit and have dominion over the earth, I believe the earth was created in the image and likeness of heaven, God's dwelling place. "The" heaven and "the" earth are actually twin planets.

Romans 1:19-20 says that we can understand the invisible things of God by examining the creation that we live in. Heaven is invisible to us in terms of our natural eyesight, but by examining the creation we can see, such as the planet we live on, I believe we can understand more about heaven. Of course, what we see here on earth is a corrupted copy because of the sin that entered the world. Nevertheless, I believe it is a copy of planet heaven.

Also, God lives in the capital city of heaven called New Jerusalem. That city isn't floating around out there in the universe somewhere. I would suggest that it's on a planet like the other cities we know about in this life. And as we've already seen, God is going to transplant His city, New Jerusalem, to earth after the earth has been renovated by fire, right before we begin living in the eternal ages to come. In reality, He'll simply be transporting it from one planet to another.

What I'm saying is probably contrary to many religious ideas stuck in your head. But you have to realize the Bible never teaches that heaven is some nebulous figment of your imagination where you retire for eternity, lay in a hammock, and sip papaya juice. Heaven is a very real place. In the same breath heaven was created, the earth was created and we know what the earth is. It's appropriate to assume since we're created in the image and likeness of God and occupy the earth, the earth is in the image and likeness of heaven, which is the present dwelling place of God.

Now, if we think back to Jesus' glorified body, His body had the capacity to move instantly between planet earth and planet heaven. How do we know this? Because Jesus ascended to the right hand of the Father in seconds. The closest star to us is hundreds of millions of light years away. If Jesus was traveling at the speed of light, He'd still be enroute to His destination today—but we know He's already there. When the disciples watched Jesus' glorified body ascend into the clouds, His body somehow had the capacity to transcend vast amounts of space in just the passage of thought. (If you thought Captain Kirk had a neat way of transportation, just wait until you experience this!) I'm not sure what you call this capability, but I know it will be amazing.

One of the reasons this transportation capability will be important is because our mansions are going to be in New Jerusalem on planet earth after God has transplanted the capital city of heaven to earth. That's where our dwelling place will be, but that's not where we will work. We'll commute. We'll be able to cover vast amounts of space in an eye blink of time. Personally, I don't plan on ruling over one or two solar systems; I'm believing for a couple galaxies somewhere to the south. And that's why my body will be able to traverse great amounts of distance, naturally speaking.

Can you see how our glorified bodies will be a great help in accomplishing our eternal assignment?

Chapter 8

Preparing Now for Your Eternal Destiny

Talking about these things can easily blow the natural mind away. That's why I'm glad Paul wrote in 1 Corinthians 2:9:

> But as it is written, Eye hath not seen, nor ear heard, neither have entered into the heart of man, the things which God hath prepared for them that love him.

This is one of my favorite verses in the Bible. God doesn't want you to be boxed in by the smallness of your mind. God's plan for your life is beyond your comprehension. I love imagining the possibilities of what God has planned for me, even though I know I'll never come close to imagining how wonderful it will be!

I encourage you to do the same. Set aside any religious ideas you may have and see the possibilities. See the big picture and the things God is preparing you for. Let the Holy Spirit show you the magnificence of what lies ahead. If you do this, it puts the daily challenges you face into proper perspective. Carnality falls by the wayside when you have the big picture of who you are in Christ and God's bigger purpose for your life. When some guy says something nasty about your tie not matching your coat, the big picture puts it in perspective. You don't have a reason to get offended when somebody doesn't like your hair style.

I'm glad the Lord has said He'll never leave us in the midst of our training here. He'll never forsake us (Hebrews 13:5). He won't let us have a training accident that ruins everything. He's going to be there, watching as we step out in faith, watching as we walk out the principles of God's Word, and then learn from what happens. He'll be our safety net.

One of the ways we are trained is by simply going through the daily challenges life brings our way. For example, our ministry has faced some challenges over the past few years, and I've learned a lot as I've prayed and asked God how to handle each one. Even though I'd rather have learned those lessons by the revelation of the Holy Spirit, a lot of lessons are often better learned when you and I walk through the test ourselves and directly confront the resistance to the unfolding will of God for our lives.

This is what prepares us for eternity. The challenges and decisions we face on this earth are opportunities to learn how to govern and be a steward on God's behalf for the eternal ages to come. The extent and nature of your eternal destiny is going to be decided by your effectiveness as God's steward on this earth. Did you produce an increase for the kingdom of God? Did you use your life's resource—your time, your talent, your money—to increase God's kingdom on this earth? The answers to those questions determine your eternal ruling assignments.

The parable of the talents in Matthew 25 is an example of this truth. The master goes on a journey to a far country and entrusts his belongings to his three servants. (This is a type of Jesus ascending to heaven to be seated at the right hand of the Father, while we oversee the work here on earth until His return.)

Two of the servants invested their portions and brought increase to the master, while the third hid his portion in the ground. When the master returned, the servants had to give an account for what they had done while he was gone.

The master said to the two who had brought increase to his kingdom, "Well done, thou good and faithful servant: thou hast been faithful over a few things, I will make thee ruler over many things: enter thou into the joy of thy lord" (Matthew 25:21).

The extent of your eternal rulership depends on how faithful you are to use the resources He has entrusted to you now to bring an increase to His kingdom in this earth. You cannot read that parable any other way.

How faithful have you been to produce increase in the kingdom of God? Are you using your time, talents, gifts, and financial resource to bring increase to the kingdom of God? Whatever your calling, whatever your vocation, no matter how many gifts and talents you think you have (or don't have), you have a responsibility to use whatever you have for God's kingdom. Remember, the guy who had five talents received the same reward as the guy who had two talents because both of them produced the same proportional increase. God simply wants you to use what you've been given for His kingdom.

Recognizing this responsibility to increase God's kingdom doesn't come naturally. When I went to college, I didn't have a concept of the big picture of life. I was in school to have as good a time as I could, make reasonably decent grades, and get out of there. That's all I wanted.

Not everyone had that view. Some who were more mature than I viewed college as a time of preparation for their future. Because of their mindset, they got out of college considerably further down the road than I did.

The same is true for us. If you only view your life as a time to have a few parties, enjoy life a little, and escape as much suffering as possible, you're going to miss out. But if you take time to view your life on earth as your opportunity to prepare for eternity, you'll position yourself much better off, not only for this life but your eternal destiny.

Strangers on This Earth

So the question really becomes, how do you do this? How can you become mindful of end-time events? How can you become aware of your eternal destiny and let that impact your life appropriately here on earth?

Hebrews 11:13 shows us how our fathers in the faith handled this question:

> *These all died in faith, not having received the promises, but having seen them afar off, and were persuaded of them, and embraced them, and confessed that they were strangers and pilgrims on the earth.*

The first time I read this verse, I was puzzled. "Wait a minute. These faith heroes died without receiving the promises. But isn't that what faith is—receiving the promises of God?"

Then it occurred to me that these people had received the promises I was thinking about. God's promises of provision and health had certainly been realized in their lives. Abraham was the richest man of his day, lived to be over 170 years old, and fathered children at the age of 130. These promises had certainly become reality in his life.

What promises hadn't they received yet?

The rest of the verse provides our answer. They saw the promises afar off, were persuaded of them, embraced them, and "confessed that they were strangers and pilgrims on the earth."

These faith heroes understood that their destinies transcended this earthly life. Their lives on earth were just an eye blink, only short seasons in the eternal scheme of things. Verses 14-16 continue:

> *For they that say such things declare plainly that they seek a country. And truly, if they had been mindful of that country from whence they came out, they might have had opportunity to have returned. But now they desire a better country, that is, an heavenly: wherefore God is not ashamed to be called their God: for he hath prepared for them a city.*

These people knew they were strangers on this earth. They knew they had destinies that were not bound by time or geographical limitation. They understood that their destinies weren't earthbound, and therefore, they considered themselves strangers. That's what made them faith heroes.

How did they do this? I think a key phrase is "if they had been mindful." If they had been mindful of this temporal world, they could have become inhabitants of it instead of acting as strangers and pilgrims looking for a better home. They, instead, were mindful of and thinking about their heavenly home.

The same is still true today. What you are mindful of creates a desire within you. If you are intensely mindful of what is going on in the world and your biggest reality is bound by natural life as defined by CNN or Fox News, then you will live in that world. That will be your big picture.

On the other hand, if you become more and more mindful of God's picture and God's eternal purpose for you, that desire begins to supersede your desire to go to the football game, your desire to go flying or play golf. It keeps you focused on God and on seeking His plan for your life.

Recognize you are a stranger in this life. Dream about ruling and reigning with Jesus. See yourself walking out His plan both on earth and in eternity, and you'll ultimately find yourself taking steps in that direction.

Living Right in These Last Days

It truly is an honor to be a part of this generation. (I guarantee you some Old Testament saints are looking over the balcony rail of heaven right now who would love to live in the day we're living!) We get to see the culmination of all things that have been prophesied regarding the redemptive work of our Lord. We get to see the close of the church age.

The fact that you are living at this point in time is not a coincidence or a mistake. God knows your gifts and talents and has a specific purpose for you to fulfill. You've been entrusted with significant responsibilities that no one else can accomplish the same way you can.

And that's why I encourage you to take time to think about the things I've laid out in this book. Imagine the possibilities. See yourself walking out the call of God on your life and living out a bright future of ruling and reigning with Jesus.

Prayer of Salvation

A born again, committed relationship with God is the key to a victorious life. Jesus, the Son of God, laid down His life and rose again so that we could spend eternity with Him in heaven and experience His absolute best on earth. The Bible says, "For God so loved the world, that he gave his only begotten Son, that whosoever believeth in him should not perish, but have everlasting life" (John 3:16).

It is the will of God that everyone receive eternal salvation. The way to receive this salvation is to call upon the name of Jesus and confess Him as your Lord. The Bible says, "That if thou shalt confess with thy mouth the Lord Jesus, and shalt believe in thine heart that God hath raised him from the dead, thou shalt be saved. For whosoever shall call upon the name of the Lord shall be saved" (Romans 10:9, 13).

Jesus has given salvation, healing, and countless benefits to all who call upon His name. These benefits can be yours if you receive Him into your heart by praying this prayer:

> *Heavenly Father, I come to You admitting that I am a sinner. Right now, I choose to turn away from sin, and I ask You to cleanse me of all unrighteousness. I believe that Your Son, Jesus, died on the cross to take away my sins. I also believe that He rose again from the dead so that I may be justified and made righteous through faith in Him. I call upon the name of Jesus Christ to be the Savior and Lord of my life. Jesus, I choose to follow You, and I ask that You fill me with the power of the Holy Spirit. I declare right now that I am a born again child of God. I am free*

from sin and full of the righteousness of God. I am saved in Jesus' name, amen.

If you have just received Jesus Christ as your Savior, or if this book has changed your life, we would like to hear from you. Please write us at:

Mac Hammond Ministries
PO Box 29469
Minneapolis, MN 55429-2946

You can also visit us on the web at
mac-hammond.org.

References

Hill, Harold. *From Goo to You by Way of the Zoo.* New Jersey: Fleming H. Revell Company, 1985.

Strong, James. *Abingdon's Strong's Exhaustive Concordance of the Bible.* "Dictionary of the Hebrew Bible." (Nashville: Abingdon Press, 1890).

Endnotes

Chapter 3

1. Hill, p. 44.
2. Hill, p. 46-47.
3. Strong, "Hebrew," entry #8414, p. 123.
4. Strong, "Hebrew," entry #1961, p. 32.

Chapter 8

1. Strong, "Hebrew," entry #8104, p. 118.

About The Author

 Mac Hammond is senior pastor of Living Word Christian Center, a large and growing body of Christian believers in Brooklyn Park (a suburb of Minneapolis), Minnesota. He is the host of the Winner's Way broadcast and author of several internationally distributed books. Mac is broadly acclaimed for his ability to apply the principles of the Bible to practical situations and the challenges of daily living.

Mac Hammond graduated from Virginia Military Institute in 1965 with a Bachelor's degree in English. Upon graduation, he entered the Air Force with a regular officer's commission and reported for pilot training at Moody Air Force Base in Georgia. He received his wings in November 1966, and subsequently served two tours of duty in Southeast Asia, accumulating 198 combat missions. He was honorably discharged in 1970 with the rank of Captain.

Between 1970 and 1980, Mac was involved in varying capacities in the general aviation industry including ownership of a successful air cargo business serving the Midwestern United States. A business acquisition brought the Hammonds to Minneapolis where they ultimately founded Living Word Christian Center in 1980 with 12 people in attendance.

That group of twelve people has grown into an active church body of 10,000 members. Today some of the outreaches that spring from Living Word include Maranatha Christian Academy, a fully-accredited, pre-K through 12th grade Christian school; Living Free Recovery Services, a state licensed outpatient treatment facility for chemical dependency; The Wells at 7th Street, a multi-faceted outreach to inner-city residents; CFAITH, an online cooperative missionary outreach of hundreds of national and international organizations providing faith-based content; and a national and international media outreach that includes hundreds of audio/video teaching series, the Winner's Way broadcast, the PrayerNotes e-newsletter, and the Winner's Way e-magazine.

To contact Mac Hammond, please write to:

Mac Hammond Ministries
PO Box 29469
Minneapolis, MN 55429-2946

Or visit us online at
mac-hammond.org

OTHER BOOKS BY MAC HAMMOND

Angels at Your Service
Releasing the Power of Heaven's Host

Doorways to Deception
How Deception Comes, How It Destroys, and How You Can Avoid It

Following the Fire
Discerning How God Leads You by the Desires of Your Heart

Heirs Together
Solving the Mystery of a Satisfying Marriage

The Last Millennium
A Revealing Look at the Remarkable Days Ahead and How You Can Live Them to the Fullest

Living Safely in a Dangerous World
Keys to Abiding in the Secret Place

Plugged In and Prospering
Embracing the Spiritual Significance and Biblical Basis for the Local Church

Positioned for Promotion
How to Increase Your Influence and Capacity to Lead

Real Faith Never Fails
Detecting (and Correcting) Four Common Faith Mistakes

Simplifying Your Life
Divine Insights to Uncomplicated Living

Soul Control
Whoever Controls Your Soul, Controls Your Destiny

The Suffering Question
Biblical Insights Into Why Bad Things Happen to Good People

Water, Wind, & Fire
Understanding the New Birth and the Baptism of the Holy Spirit

Water, Wind, & Fire—The Next Steps
Developing Your New Relationship With God

The Way of the Winner
Running the Race to Victory

Who God Is Not
Exploding the Myths About His Nature and His Ways

Winning In Your Finances
How to Walk God's Pathway to Prosperity

Winning Your World
Becoming a Person of Influence

Yielded and Bold
How to Understand and Flow With the Move of God's Spirit

OTHER BOOKS BY MAC AND LYNNE HAMMOND

Keys to Compatibility
Opening the Door to a Marvelous Marriage

Other Books by Lynne Hammond

Dare to Be Free!

Devotions for the Praying Heart: Prayer Notes

Heaven's Power for the Harvest
Be Part of God's End-Time Spiritual Outpouring

Living in the Presence of God
Receive Joy, Peace, and Direction in the Secret Place of Prayer

Love and Devotion
Prayer Journal

The Master Is Calling
Discovering the Wonders of Spirit-Led Prayer

The Master Is Calling Workbook
Discovering the Wonders of Spirit-Led Prayer

Renewed in His Presence
Satisfying Your Hunger for God

Secrets to Powerful Prayer
Discovering the Languages of the Heart

Staying Faith
How to Stand Until the Answer Arrives

The Table of Blessing
Recipes From the Family and Friends of Living Word Christian Center

When Healing Doesn't Come Easily

When It's Time for a Miracle
The Hour of Impossible Breakthroughs Is Now!

Whispers From the Secret Place
A 31-day Journey

For a catalog of our books, CDs,
and DVDs, please contact us at:

Mac Hammond Ministries
PO Box 29469
Minneapolis, MN 55429-2946

You can also visit us on the web at
mac-hammond.org.